Greater Than   Book
Series
Reviews from Readers

I think the series is wonderful and beneficial for tourists to get information before visiting the city.

-Seckin Zumbul, Izmir Turkey

I am a world traveler who has read many trip guides but this one really made a difference for me. I would call it a heartfelt creation of a local guide expert instead of just a guide.

-Susy, Isla Holbox, Mexico

New to the area like me, this is a must have!

-Joe, Bloomington, USA

This is a good series that gets down to it when looking for things to do at your destination without having to read a novel for just a few ideas.

-Rachel, Monterey, USA

Good information to have to plan my trip to this destination.

-Pennie Farrell, Mexico

Great ideas for a port day.

-Mary Martin USA

Aptly titled, you won't just be a tourist after reading this book. You'll be greater than a tourist!

-Alan Warner, Grand Rapids, USA

Even though I only have three days to spend in San Miguel in an upcoming visit, I will use the author's suggestions to guide some of my time there. An easy read - with chapters named to guide me in directions I want to go.

 -Robert Catapano, USA

Great insights from a local perspective! Useful information and a very good value!

 -Sarah, USA

This series provides an in-depth experience through the eyes of a local. Reading these series will help you to travel the city in with confidence and it'll make your journey a unique one.

-Andrew Teoh, Ipoh, Malaysia

GREATER THAN A TOURIST-
MINUTE MAN NATIONAL HISTORICAL PARK MASSACHUSETTS USA

50 Travel Tips from a Local

Kevin Vincent

Cover designed by: Ivana Stamenkovic
Cover Image:
https://commons.wikimedia.org/wiki/File:Old_North_Bridge,_Concord,_Massac husetts,_July_2005.JPG Daderot at en.wikipedia / CC BY-SA (http://creativecommons.org/licenses/by-sa/3.0/)

Image 1: https://en.wikipedia.org/wiki/File:Hartwell_Tavern_2.jpeg
Image 2:
https://commons.wikimedia.org/wiki/File:Minute_Man,_Daniel_Chester_French,_Concord_ MA.jpg Daniel Chester French / Public domain
Image 3:
https://commons.wikimedia.org/wiki/File:The_Wayside_Concord_Massachusetts.jpg
Daderot at English Wikipedia / CC BY-SA (http://creativecommons.org/licenses/by-sa/3.0/)
Image 4:
https://commons.wikimedia.org/wiki/File:Captain_William_Smith_House,_Lincoln_MA.jpg
John Phelan / CC BY (https://creativecommons.org/licenses/by/3.0)

CZYK Publishing Since 2011.
Greater Than a Tourist

Lock Haven, PA
All rights reserved.

ISBN: 9798643250203

>TOURIST

50 TRAVEL TIPS FROM A LOCAL

BOOK DESCRIPTION

With travel tips and culture in our guidebooks written by a local, it is never too late to visit Minute Man National Park. Greater Than a Tourist - Minute Man National Historical Park by Author Kevin Vincent offers the inside scoop on the home of the "shot heard around the world" and birthplace of the American Revolution. Most travel books tell you how to travel like a tourist. Although there is nothing wrong with that, as part of the 'Greater Than a Tourist' series, this book will give you candid travel tips from someone who has lived at your next travel destination. This guide book will not tell you exact addresses or store hours but instead gives you knowledge that you may not find in other smaller print travel books. Experience cultural, culinary delights, and attractions with the guidance of a Local. Slow down and get to know the people with this invaluable guide. By the time you finish this book, you will be eager and prepared to discover new activities at your next travel destination.

Inside this travel guide book you will find:

Visitor information from a Local
Tour ideas and inspiration
Save time with valuable guidebook information

Greater Than a Tourist- A Travel Guidebook with 50 Travel Tips from a Local. Slow down, stay in one place, and get to know the people and culture. By the time you finish this book, you will be eager and prepared to travel to your next destination.

OUR STORY

Traveling is a passion of the Greater than a Tourist book series creator. Lisa studied abroad in college, and for their honeymoon Lisa and her husband toured Europe. During her travels to Malta, an older man tried to give her some advice based on his own experience living on the island since he was a young boy. She was not sure if she should talk to the stranger but was interested in his advice. When traveling to some places she was wary to talk to locals because she was afraid that they weren't being genuine. Through her travels, Lisa learned how much locals had to share with tourists. Lisa created the Greater Than a Tourist book series to help connect people with locals. A topic that locals are very passionate about sharing.

TABLE OF CONTENTS

ABOUT THE AUTHOR

Kevin Vincent is an author and dog-daycare worker who lives in Massachusetts. Kevin is a local who knows the towns including Lexington and Concord. He loves comic books, dogs and history, especially the American Revolution!

HOW TO USE THIS BOOK

The *Greater Than a Tourist* book series was written by someone who has lived in an area for over three months. The goal of this book is to help travelers either dream or experience different locations by providing opinions from a local. The author has made suggestions based on their own experiences. Please check before traveling to the area in case the suggested places are unavailable.

Travel Advisories: As a first step in planning any trip abroad, check the Travel Advisories for your intended destination.
https://travel.state.gov/content/travel/en/traveladvisories/traveladvisories.html

FROM THE PUBLISHER

Traveling can be one of the most important parts of a person's life. The anticipation and memories that you have are some of the best. As a publisher of the Greater Than a Tourist, as well as the popular *50 Things to Know* book series, we strive to help you learn about new places, spark your imagination, and inspire you. Wherever you are and whatever you do I wish you safe, fun, and inspiring travel.

Lisa Rusczyk Ed. D.
CZYK Publishing

WELCOME TO
> TOURIST

Hartwell Tavern, Lincoln, Massachusetts

The Minute Man

The Wayside, Concord, Massachusetts. Home to Louisa May Alcott and her sisters, Nathaniel Hawthorne, and Margaret Sidney, creator of the "Five Little Peppers"

Captain William Smith House, Lincoln Massachusetts

*"Stand your ground. Don't fire
unless fired upon, but if they mean
to have a war let it begin here."*

- Captain James Parker on the morning of April
19, 1775

L exington and Concord, Massachusetts are home to the birth of the American Revolution. Minute Man National Historical Park brings to life the sacrifice and history made throughout the area. Included are the great American authors Nathaniel Hawthorne and Harriett Lothrop who lived at the Wayside. Walk along Battle Road Trail, in the footsteps of the British soldiers and militia-men hiding among the forest. At Minute Man National Park you breathe history.

Minute Man NHP
Massachusetts
Climate

	High	Low
January	36	18
February	38	20
March	45	28
April	58	39
May	68	49
June	78	59
July	83	64
August	82	62
September	73	54
October	63	43
November	51	34
December	39	23

GreaterThanaTourist.com

Temperatures are in Fahrenheit degrees.
Source: NOAA

1. PRECEDING THE REVOLUTIONARY WAR

The French and Indian War started in 1756 and lasted until 1763 and is also known as The Seven Years War. This would be another conflict in the New World with the British colonies and the ambitions of New France to expand their territory into the Ohio valley (from north in Canada). Between 1754 and 1755, preceding the official declaration of War from the British, the French won a string of victories at and nearby Fort Duquesne. The French defeated a young George Washington, Edward Braddock and William Shirley in quick-succession. In 1756 the British formally declared war on France. They would not see success until 1757 when the new leader, William Pitt, saw the colonies as crucial to building a British empire. He would borrow from Prussia to raise troops in the colonies and home. By 1758 the British claimed two major victories at Louisbourg and Fort Frontenac. The British would go on to win a major victory at the Battle of Quebec under General James Wolfe in 1759. Both he and the French commander, Montcalm were mortally injured. The War would continue with Britain conquering French acquisitions in the New World after losing their canadian foothold. The Treaty of Paris in February of 1763 would see an end to the war but at great financial cost overall to both Britain and France. Britain would see her national debt doubled after the end of the conflict. Additionally, King George III would install permanent British army garrisons in the American colonies to protect from further attacks.

"No taxation without representation" stands as the reason for the beginning of the American Revolution. Following the French and Indian War, Great Britain saw itself in debt and used the American colonies as a source of revenue. Two British laws including: The Stamp Act (March, 1765) and The Townshend Acts (June 1967) led to rising colonist unrest. The first taxed transactions throughout the colonies on a never-before-seen scale. The latter passed taxes on British goods being imported into the colonies. For the first time, a board of custom officials were instituted to further extend the Crown's rule.

2. BOSTON MASSACRE

At the beginning of the 1700 2,000 British soldiers were garrisoned in Boston and the tension was palpable. Colonists who supported the Crown, loyalists, found themselves frequently at violent odds with their fellow colonists who saw themselves as patriots. The death of eleven year old Christopher Seider only further exacerbated the tension. On March 5, 1770 the tension erupted in violence at the Custom House located at King Street, Boston. A riot broke out after a British soldier accidentally injured a colonist with his bayonet. The crowd responded with force and an alarm broke out summoning additional British soldiers. British regulars with muskets and bayonets take a defensive position outside of the Custom House. A crowd of colonists hurl rocks, snow and glass at the soldiers. Gunfire broke out and after the smoke settled 5 colonists were killed. Their deaths further promoted the cause of the patriots but both sides used the event as means of propaganda. The Boston Massacre further polarized the American colonists from the loyalists and British soldiers.

3. BOSTON TEA PARTY

The Townshend Acts of 1767 taxed essentials such as tea, paint and paper. The British denied any colonist representation in Parliament further angering them. On December 16, 1773 at Griffin's Wharf patriots part of the Sons of Liberty dumped 342 chests of tea from the British East India Company into the Boston Harbor. Samuel Adams, Paul Revere and William Molineux were three of the most well-known. Great Britain passed the Coercive (Intolerable) Acts in summer of 1774 as a direct response. The Boston Tea Party invoked a strict and devastating retaliation from the British setting up what would become the Revolutionary War.

4. CONCORD, MASSACHUSETTS

The town of Concord was established in 1635 by a small group of British settlers. It became home to a group of authors centered around Ralph Waldo Emerson and included Nathaniel Hawthorne. The original Algonquin name, "Musketaquid," means "grassy plain" and the settlers named it Concord after the peaceful negotiations between English and the Algonquin tribe settled there. Concord has a population of about 18,000 and a motto of: "How Strong Is Harmony." The Old North Bridge stands in Concord as one of the key battle locations of April 19, 1775. Concord is home to one of the most influential literary generations including Ralph Waldo

Emerson, Louisa Alcott and Henry David Thoreau. Particular points of interest include Walden Pond, Cyrus Pierce House and the Wheeler-Minot Farmhouse. In 1853 a Concord farmer, Ephraim Bull started selling the Concord grape. To this day, Welch's Grape Juice calls Concord home.

5. LEXINGTON, MASSACHUSETTS

Lexington, Massachusetts was settled in 1642 and primarily consisted of farmland. Cambridge originally made up the town but became separate in 1713. The name Lexington remains a bit of a controversy. Either it came from Lord Lexington a noble in England or was named after Lexington, England (present-day Nottinghamshire, England). Around 33,000 live in Lexington in what is now Middlesex county. The town motto reads: "What a glorious morning for America!" One of the most famous landmarks in Lexington is of course the town green and also the Old Belfry. Erected in 1761, it rang out the call-to-arms to Captain Parker's militia the morning of April 19, 1775. The original was destroyed by high winds in 1909 and was rebuilt in 1910. In addition to Minute Man National Historical Park, Lexington is home to the Willards Woods Conservation Area, The Scottish Rite Masonic Museum and the Old Burying Ground.

6. LEXINGTON BATTLE GREEN

On April 19, 1775 at roughly 4:30 a.m. in the morning, the first shots of the Revolutionary War were fired at the Lexington Common. Now known as the Lexington Battle Green, local militia and British regulars engaged in battle. The British company heavily outnumbered the colonists although both sides suffered heavy casualties. Roughly 400 British regulars confronted 77 Massachusetts militia. Of the 77, 49 were killed and 39 injured with several others missing. On the British side, 73 were killed and 174 were wounded. The British pushed back the colonists and moved onward to Concord and its weapons caches.

Present day the Lexington Battle Green annually on Patriot's Day hosts one of the larger reenactments complete with musket-firing, bayonets and horseback cavalry. The Lexington Common is a National Historic Landmark designated on January 20, 1961. Throughout April you can take guided tours of the area including the graves where 7 patriots rest. You will find the statue of Captain John Parker and the Revolutionary Monument commemorating the lives lost.

7. CREATION OF THE PARK

Minute Man National Historical Park was established on September 21, 1959 under the National Park Service. The 970 acres of land include parts of Lexington, Concord and Lincoln, Massachusetts. David Vela is the current Deputy Director of the National Park Service and oversees the more than 20,000 employees nationwide. In addition, over 300,000 volunteers work in national parks and sites throughout the country. President Woodrow Wilson established the NPS on August 25, 1916. Minute Man National Historical Park follows the Battle of Lexington and Concord. The 5 mile "Battle Road Trail" serves as one of the highlights of the park from the onset as well as Concord's Old North Bridge. Taverns, homesteads trails and battlefields make up the park itself. The Minute Man Visitor Center and the North Bridge Visitor Center are the two best places to start your journey through April 1775 and the birth of our nation.

8. MINUTE MAN VISITOR CENTER

Find the beginning of your journey through the American Revolution's birthplace at the Minute Man Visitor Center. Located at 250 Great Road North, Lincoln, Massachusetts, the center offers access to maps, guided tours and video presentations. "The Road to Revolution," shown every 30 minutes during business hours (9:00 a.m. to 4:30 p.m.), serves as a jumping point onward to the park. This presentation depicts the events leading up to and including the Battles at Lexington and Concord.

9. HANCOCK–CLARKE HOUSE

The Hancock-Clarke House sits in Lexington, Massachusetts where John Hancock lived from 1699 to 1775. On the eve of the Battles of Lexington and Concord, aware of the British company incoming, Hancock and Samuel Adams fled the area to avoid British capture. It is one of the original structures in the Minute Man National Historical Park. In 1971 the house received protected-status from the National Register of Historic Places. Like much of Minute Man National Historical Park, "Living History" demonstrations and tours make this a popular place to visit.

10. CAPTAIN PARKER STATUE

Daniel Chester French is the sculptor of the 7 foot tall bronze "Minuteman" statue at North Bridge in Concord. French was paid $1,000 for the statue unveiled on April 19, 1875. A verse from Ralph Waldo Emerson's "A Concord Hymn" is inscribed on the base: "... And fired the shot heard round the world." Near the statue stands an obelisk in memorial to those who lost their lives at the North Bridge on April 19, 1775.

The Minute Man, Captain John Parker (born July 13, 1729) led the 77 militiamen against a company of British regulars on the morning of April 19, 1775 at Lexington Green. Parker fought in the French and Indian War making him a battle-veteran before the beginning of the Revolutionary War. Seeing the size of the British company advancing on his men, Captain Parker ordered his men to retreat from Lexington Green in an attempt to save more lives. Later in the day, Captain Parker took up a position at "Parker's Revenge" and ambushed the retreating British company. The life-size statue stands on the

Lexington Green now to commemorate his life. Captain Parker and the Lexington Minute Men fought during the Siege of Boston but Parker himself was unable to fight at the Battle of Bunker Hill. Captain John Parker died from tuberculosis on September 17, 1775.

11. NORTH BRIDGE CONCORD

Following the Battle of Lexington, British regulars moved on to Concord in search of the militia arm caches. At Concord's Old North Bridge multiple minutemen companies combining for a total of 400 men attacked a British company of only about 100 men and forced them to retreat from Concord and back to Boston. Colonel James Barett's troops from the vantage point on Punkatasset Hill, saw the smoke and burning town of Concord and decided to fall back, about 300 yards from the North Bridge. When the British regulars tried to hold the North Bridge, the militia advanced and the "shot heard round the world" as penned by Ralph Waldo Emerson rang out as they returned a volley against the British regulars. The British end up having to retreat to Boston after finding no weapons caches in Concord after searching for hours. In addition to Ralph Waldo Emerson's "Concord Hymn," Amos Doolittle created infamous engravings of the Battle of Lexington and Concord.

The North Bridge or "Old North Bridge" was actually dismantled in 1793 (the town of Concord constructed a newer and more practical bridge a few yards away) and then was reconstructed multiple times, the final time being in 1909. On the 200th anniversary of the battle in 1975, President Gerald Ford traveled to Concord to commemorate the Old North Bridge. In 2005, the bridge was renovated for the final time. The bridge spans over the Concord River which runs through Minute Man National Historical Park. The remains of two British soldiers are buried at this site. A poem by their graves reads: "They came three thousand miles and died, to keep the past upon its throne, unheard beyond the ocean tide, their English Mother made her moan" (American poet, James Russell Lowell).

12. BATTLE ROAD TRAIL

Battle Road Trail runs for 4.9 miles from Fisk Hill (in the east) and Meriam's Corner in the west. The trail dissects many of the major attractions and landmarks at the Park. Battle Road Trail traces the

British retreat to Boston following the defeat at Concord. Much of the actual Battle Road itself has been paved over or developed on as you get closer to Cambridge. Many visitors to Minute Man love biking on the wide path or walking parts of the trail. On Patriot's Day weekend throughout the park volunteers reenact the battles fought along the road and engage visitors in "Living History" demonstrations. You can also join a park ranger to walk a 3.5 hour guided tour of Battle Road Trail (subject to weather and availability).

13. THE WAYSIDE

The Wayside is known as the "Home of the Authors" and sits in Concord, Massachusetts on the present Minute Man National Park grounds. Nathaniel Hawthorne and Margaret Sidney are two of the authors who lived there since the home's 1717 construction. Minute Man Samuel Whitney lived at the house in 1774 witnessing the retreating British troops from Lexington and Concord. Today visitors to the park can tour the house and even experience "Living History" demonstrations.

14. PARKER'S REVENGE

By mid-afternoon April 19, 1775 the British regular companies under Major John Pitcairn began their retreat back to Boston after clashing with a surprisingly well-trained militia. Captain John Parker and the Lexington Militia ambushed the British companies at the border of Lexington and Lincoln along what is now known as Battle Road Trail. His militia wore the bloodied bandages from the slaughter on Lexington Green earlier in the morning yet they still possessed the courage and desire to engage the British again. It became a metaphor for the entire Revolutionary War: Americans will get back up and fight every time they are knocked down.

15. MUNROE TAVERN

Munroe Tavern sits on Massachusetts Ave in Lexington, Massachusetts and served as an important building for both the Colonists and British during the battles of Lexington and Concord. The militiamen in the early morning of April 19, met at the Tavern including Captain John Parker and William Munroe himself. To this day in 2020, the Lexington Minute Men meet monthly at the Munroe Tavern. After the opening shots of the war on the Lexington Green, British regulars took over Munroe Tavern and set up a field hospital. Guests to the National Park can walk through the Tavern and experience demonstrations by costumed Park volunteers on Patriot's Day Weekend. Additionally, the Third US Infantry Regiment (serving since 1784, the oldest active-duty infantry group in the US) will play fife and drums by Munroe Tavern opposite Tower Park.

Tower Park is home to military demonstrations on Patriot's Day weekend. The Lexington Minute Men, Acton Minute Men, Tenth Regiment of Foot (British regular reenactors) and other reenactors demonstrate musket and cannon firing as well as military battle techniques. His Majesty's Tenth Regiment of Foot in America or "Tenth Regiment of Foot " complete the reenactments at Minute Man National Historical park by participating as British regulars. Founded in 1968 this American organization strives to accurately represent the Crown's army. In addition to the Tower Park Battle Demonstration and the Lexington Green reenactment, they participate in parades and reenactments in other states such as New York, Connecticut, Rhode Island and others.

16. HARTWELL TAVERN

Built in 1732, Hartwell Tavern was one of the buildings that existed before the Battles of Lexington and Concord. This is considered one of the "witness houses" found throughout the park. The tavern sits on the former "Bay Road" which follows Battle Road Trail. The British captured Paul Revere and William Dawes just up the road from the tavern on April 18, 1775. One of their party, Dr. Samuel Prescott escaped capture. Prescott went to Hartwell Tavern and told Captain William Smith of the oncoming British attack at Concord. The Lincoln Minute Men with the information of the impending attack were able to defend the Old North Bridge. On Patriot's Day weekend, volunteers dress up in costume and engage in "Living History" with visitors. The National Park Service purchased the property in 1967 and renovations on it began.

17. PAUL REVERE CAPTURE SITE

Paul Revere (1735-1818) worked for the Boston Committee of Correspondence and the Massachusetts Committee of Safety as a rider to carry important

43

messages and letters. On the orders of Dr. Joseph Warren, Revere set out from his house in Boston to warn Samuel Adams, John Hancock and the local militia of the impending British search for weapons at Concord. This would become known as "The Midnight Ride" immortalized in Henry Wadsworth Longfellow's poem, "Paul Revere's Ride" (1861). Revere traveled with William Dawes after witnessing the British regular companies departing Boston for Lexington and Concord. Dawes and Revere were eventually captured at gunpoint, not far away from Hartwell Tavern. From Revere's 1775 deposition the British regulars yell out: "If you go an Inch further, you are a dead man!" They confiscated Revere's horse and here in Concord Revere's ride would end. Dr. William Prescott, a confidant of Revere and Dawes made it to Concord where they were able to muster the militia in time.

Present-day a marker shows the spot of Paul Revere's capture. You will find it at the cross section of Massachusetts Ave and Mill Street inside Minute Man National Historical Park. On Patriot's Day Weekend the town of Concord and Minute Man National Historical Park reenact the Paul Revere Capture. First you will see the Lincoln Minute Men walking down Battle Road. Next, they will do a dramatic reading of Henry Longfellow's poem. Reenactors play Revere, Prescott, Dawes, Mary Hartwell and Henry Longfellow himself as redcoats search the area eventually capturing Revere. Additionally, in April the town of Medford reenacts Paul Revere's stop on his way to Concord, complete with a horse!

18. CAPTAIN WILLIAM SMITH HOUSE

The home of Captain William Smith sits on Battle Road in Lincoln, Massachusetts. William Smith married Catherine Louisa Salmon in 1771. The couple would settle in Lincoln three years later. Captain William Smith, in the early morning hours of April 19, 1775, sounded the alarm for the militia to respond to the British attack at Lexington and Concord. Captain Smith and the Lincoln Minute Men would successfully engage and repel the British at North Bridge as well as later in the day as they retreated to Boston. In an interesting turn of events, Captain Smith's wife, Catherine Louisa, treated a British regular for his wounds as the moving-battle passed by the Smith House. The National Park Service restored the house in 1983-1985 including the original mid-eighteenth century staircase and the 1730 lean-to. On Patriot's Day weekend the Minute Man National Historical Park hosts reenactments and guided-tours of the Captain William Smith House. One presentation sums up the experience of William Smith and Catherine Louisa titled: "Life on Battle Road." See costumed re-enactors live out everyday life in 1775 Massachusetts.

19. SAMUEL BROOKS HOUSE

The Samuel Brooks House was built approximately in 1692 and is located at the corner of Route 2A and Lexington Road in Concord. It served as a family homestead and "Witness House" to the advancing British company on April 19, 1775. Samuel Brooks drilled with the Concord militia but his family would still have been on the property. It would look incredibly scary to see columns of uniformed British regulars marching by onto Lexington and ultimately, Concord. At the edge of the Brooks family property later in the day, local militia engaged British regulars leading to skirmishes throughout the area. Records of the Concord Militia involvement on April 19, 1775 do not exist so therefore we do not decisively know if Samuel Brooks fought alongside his countrymen on the Lexington Green or at the North Bridge. After the Battles of Lexington and Concord, Samuel Brooks was drafted into the Continental Army but paid ten pounds in a "lieu" to take care of his elderly mother. In 1781 he married Mary Flint and would live until 1811.

20. BLOODY ANGLE

Hundreds of militia took up superior positions on Battle Road as the British marched 19 miles back to Boston. At the now-called Bloody Angle, Battle Road veers left, goes northeast then doglegs to the right causing a distinct "S" in the road. Concord Militia set up on the west side of the road and the Woburn militia on the east surrounding the unknowing (and already battle-weary) British company. This took a great toll on the British claiming 30 of their over 70 deaths from the day. A marker sits present-day at the Bloody Angle where two British soldiers are buried.

You can go on a tour where a costumed volunteer, Edmund Foster, takes you around the battle site. This occurs the Saturday before Patriot's Day Monday

which includes the Parker's Revenge reenactment and
Barrett House search by the British.

21. MERIAM'S CORNER

Meriam's Corner is the site where Battle Road
begins and the colonists engaged the British regulars
in guerilla warfare to great success. The militia used
their knowledge of the area to hide and ambush the
British. This set the tone for the war whereas the
British previously primarily engaged in open ground-
column based warfare. Nathan Meriam's house sits at
the corner of Bay (or Battle) Road and Bedford Road
in Concord. The father and his sons fought at the
Battle of Lexington: Josiah, Josiah Jr. and Timothy.

22. ROBBINS HOUSE

The Robbins House is considered the home and
now museum of the first generation of freed slaves in
America. It is located at 320 Monument Street in
Concord, Massachusetts it is not far from Minute
Man National Historical Park. Caesar Robbins (1745-
1822) enslaved at birth, enlisted in the Acton militia,
Captain Zacariah's 5th Company and was

emancipated after his service. Peter Hutchinson (1799-1882) was the last African American owner of the house, a distant relative to the Robbins family.

23. ELISHA JONES HOUSE

Elisha Jones (1744-1810) lived in Concord and worked as a blacksmith. He was an active member of the Concord Militia during the start of the Revolutionary War. Later, he would become a lieutenant in the Concord Light Infantry Company of the Continental Army. The Elisha Jones House is one of eleven that stood before the battles of April 19, 1775. It stands on the battlefield yet is privately owned and only viewable by street. The National Park Service defined it as a "Witness house" due to its proximity to the battlefield. Elisha Jones watched the British retreat to Boston passing over the Old North Bridge on Battle Road from his family's house. One of the British soldiers took a shot at Elisha that missed and left a hole in the family's shed.

24. OLD MANSE

The Old Manse is a now-museum on the banks of the Concord River overlooking the North Bridge. Built in 1770, the Old Manse became a home, like the Wayside, to many American authors. Ralph Waldo Emerson and Nathaniel Hawthorne both called the house home for periods of time. This property neighbors but is not actually operated by Minute Man rather the Trustees of Reservations. They offer guided tours throughout the year. Footpaths connect the Old North Bridge, the Old Manse and the boathouse on the Concord River making it a beautiful springtime walk. Find the bookstore inside selling official guides, books about the Trustees of Reservations and novels by 19th century Concord authors. Nathaniel Hawthorne would write Mosses from an Old Manse here, a tribute to the homestead and beautiful nature that surrounds it. Ralph Waldo Emerson wrote Nature in the upstairs study of the Old Manse. The collection of authors who came to both reside and write in Concord centered their writing on nature and what would come to be called: American Transcendentalism. This is the concept of temporarily replacing common sense with imagination often interwoven with themes relating to nature.

25. CONCORD MUSEUM

Concord Museum is a privately owned museum, independent of Minute Man National Historical Park, but stands mere feet away. The museum was founded in 1886 and as its mission states, "... historic Concord, Massachusetts houses one of the oldest and most treasured collections of Americana in the country." You will find many interesting pieces of history here including: the lantern used for the "one if by land and two if by sea" signaling on the night of April 18, 1775, a collection of David Henry Thoreau writings and American Revolution artifacts like cannonballs. At the Rasmussen Education Center sit in on lectures and programs designed to further dive into the 1770s. One exhibition at Concord Museum "Beyond Midnight: Paul Revere and his Ride," takes a look into the night of April 18, 1775 and what led up to and followed it. Plan about 45 minutes to an hour to see Concord Museum's highlights (potentially longer if you wish to see a presentation)!

26. BARRETT HOUSE

James Barrett (born on July 31, 1710 and died on April 11, 1779) would play a crucial role in the events of April 19, 1775. He served as a Captain in the French and Indian War and after coming home would join the Concord Militia. Additionally, he served as Concord's delegate to the newly formed Provincial Congress. In 1774, he was commissioned Colonel in command of the Middlesex Militia Regiment.

Colonel James Barrett's house was built in 1705 and is roughly 2 miles from the North Bridge. The Barrett family played a major role in the events of April 19. Colonel Barrett was commissioned by the Provincial Congress to secure munitions before the incoming British advance. He and his compatriots hid heavy artillery and weaponry around his farm and around the town. In particular, two pairs of bronze cannons would be crucial to the patriot's efforts. After the skirmish at Lexington, British moved onto Concord and searched for weapons but found none thanks to the diligence of Barrett and his allies.

The Saturday before Patriot's Day you can go to Barrett House to see the "warlike preparations" for the impending British attack. Re-enactors will hide weaponry and you can even join in on the fun and help! On the Sunday before Patriot's Day annually, British soldiers search the Barrett House looking for weaponry. This event is open to the public and includes Sudbury Militia re-enactors and costumed park volunteers.

27. MAJOR JOHN BUTTRICK HOUSE

Major John Buttrick (1731-1791) served in the Concord Militia as one of its first leaders. According to "A Concord Hymn" he is the man who fired the "shot heard around the world." After the Battle of Concord he fought at the Siege of Boston under Colonel John Nixon and would go on to serve at the Battle of Saratoga. John Buttrick served as a Concord town selectman after the war. He passed in 1791 and lived his last days in the house that bears his family name.

The Major John Buttrick House stands at Liberty St. in Concord and was built in 1710. Used now for park staff housing after being bought by the National Park Service in 1962. It is one of eleven "witness houses" in the park that stood before and after the Battles of Lexington and Concord. Major John

Buttrick led the militia against the British attack at Concord's North Bridge.

28. NATIVE PLANTS AND ANIMALS

Minute Man is home to many species of plants and animals that one commonly finds in Massachusetts as a whole. In the park, 250 different species of plants have been documented. Dominant species of trees include sugar maple, silver maple, white oak and American beech. Throughout the park you will find bodies of water including ponds and wetlands (forested and emergent). The main wetlands are at the North Bridge unit, Wayside unit and along Battle Road. At Minute Man, 70 species of birds, 12 species of fish, 30 species of reptiles and amphibians have been documented. You will also find Eastern cottontail, gray squirrel, red fox, white-taled deer and more mammals. Minute Man National Historical Park is designed to enhance and indulge the beauty of the natural landscape comprising it.

29. LIBERTY RIDE

The Liberty Ride, at the Lexington Visitor Center, offers trolley rides of historic Lexington and Concord. Located at 1605 Massachusetts Ave in Lexington this tour will take you down Battle Road and other historic sites from April 19, 1775. The tour's first destination is the Lexington Battle Green. Then you will head to the Minute Man National Historical Park starting at the Visitor Center and the Paul Revere Capture Site. Ride along Battle Road seeing Meriam's Corner. Continuing down Battle Road the tour will head to Concord's North Bridge. Your tour guide dressed in an authentic 1770s wardrobe will give you all the best information about each area. Independent of Minute Man, but great to do in the area, the Liberty Ride gives guests a 90 minute tour of Lexington and Concord. Open seasonal: weekends through April and May, daily from Memorial Day until the last weekend in October.

30. SLEEPY HOLLOW CEMETERY

Sleepy Hollow Cemetery is at 34A Bedford St, Concord, Massachusetts and was established in 1855.

It stands as one of the oldest public cemeteries in the United States. At Sleepy Hollow Cemetery you will find Author's Ridge: the gravesites of Ralph Waldo Emerson, Nathaniel and Sophia Hawthorne (The Scarlet Letter), Henry David Thoreau (Walden) and Harriet Lothrop (St. George and the Dragon) all lie here. You also will find the Melvin Memorial at Sleepy Hollow Cemetery. David Chester French, architect behind the Lincoln Memorial in Washington D.C., sculpted the Melvin Memorial. Also known as the "Mourning victory" it remembers the lives of three brothers lost in the Civil War. In 1931 French himself would be buried at Sleepy Hollow Cemetery. The cemetery was dedicated by Ralph Waldo Emerson on September 29, 1855 who called it the "garden of the living" connecting the monuments to the natural landscape surrounding them.

31. EFFECTS OF LEXINGTON AND CONCORD – BUNKER HILL

The Siege of Boston started on April 19, 1775 following the British retreat from Lexington and Concord and lasted until March 17, 1776. This was crucial to the early stages of the War because the

British Army was garrisoned in Boston. Israel Putnam, William Prescott and the colonist militiamen used cannons to fortify Dorchester Heights giving them tactical superiority over the harbor and city. Around 5,500 men were engaged in the Battle of Bunker Hill making it the largest of the war thus far.

On June 14, 1775 the Continental Congress instituted the Continental Army with George Washington as the new Commander in Chief. Only 3 days later on June 17, 1775 the siege hit a climax with the Battle of Bunker Hill at Charlestown. At Breed's Hill adjacent to Bunker Hill and where the majority of the fighting took place, about 1,000 men in the Continental Army under Colonel William Prescott held off countless British advances trying to take the position. Eventually the British took the position, although at an incredibly high cost. The colonists were forced to retreat to Cambridge ending the battle. The British reported over a 1,000 casualties with 226 dead and more than 800 wounded. Major Pitcairn himself died from his wounds at Breed's Hill on June 17. The colonist militia under Prescott and Gage suffered 305 wounded and 115 killed. The Battle of Bunker Hill was won by the British but demonstrated the nature of the war - it would be long and difficult. The surprising resolve of the newly formed

Continental Army supplemented by local militia combined with their ability to return uniformed volleys at the British set the tone of the war that would last until 1783. Pitcairn saw the colonists as merely farmers on the Lexington Green - this was clearly not the case.

32. CONTINUED EFFECTS OF APRIL 19, 1775

The Battle for Fort Ticonderoga and the Battle of Quebec both show the continued effects of the Battles of Lexington and Concord. On May 10, 1775 the colonist militia under General Benedict Arnold and Major General Ethan Allen took over the stronghold of Fort Ticonderoga in northern New York. The Green Mountain Boys and other New York militia fought in the battle. This proved a crucial victory for the colonists early in the war. They are able to use British weaponry garrisoned there for the ongoing Siege of Boston. It was however, taken back in June of that year 2 months later by General John Burgoyne and the British did not abandon it until the Saratoga campaign in 1781. Fort Ticonderoga's artillery reserves and other weaponry allowed the colonists to begin what they started at Lexington and Concord.

After Fort Ticonderoga fell, with momentum on their side, the Green Mountain Boys led by Ethan Allan attempted to take Montreal (September of 1775) by themselves (around 100 men). This resulted in a major failure that Allan himself was captured; the American invasion of Canada was off to a terrible start. The American response to defeat would be to send two of their major generals: Benedict Arnold and Richard Montgomery, to take Quebec. General Benedict Arnold would take the southern approach going around New England and Major General Richard Montgomery led the forces in the north to surround Quebec. In December of 1775 on New Year's Eve the Battle of Quebec broke out. The Continental Army, about 1200 men, laid siege to Quebec. They would suffer 515 casualties with 50 killed and 400 plus missing or captured. The British led by General Guy Carleton (the then Provincial Governor of Quebec) and 1,800 men held the city and defeated the colonists for the first time in a major battle (since the opening skirmish at Lexington).

33. DECLARATION OF INDEPENDENCE

The Battles of Lexington and Concord on April 19, 1775 would set in motion the Revolutionary War and penultimately the Declaration of Independence two years later. Thomas Jefferson would write the Declaration of Independence following his 1774 publication: "A Summary View of the Rights of British America." In this, he laid out the grievances of the colonists to the First Continental Congress and ultimately to King George III. For the first time in writing Jefferson argued that the British Parliament did not possess the right to govern the colonies. In mid-June of 1776 a five man committee were commissioned by the Continental Congress to write formal articles of declaration: Thomas Jefferson, John Adams, Benjamin Franklin, Roger Sherman and Robert Livingston. On July 4, 1776 the Continental Congress formally adopted the Declaration of Independence in Philadelphia.

34. VOLUNTEERING

Minute Man National Historical Park relies on passionate volunteers to help make it function properly. Visitor Guides help keep the public oriented throughout the park, usually these are the first park officials visitors to Minute Man will see. They provide maps, suggestions to different destinations in the park and answer visitor questions. As a History Interpreter learn about specific locations in the park to present programs to visitors. These locations include North Bridge, Meriam's Corner, Capt. William Smith House, Bloody Angle, Parker's Revenge, Whittemore House. As a Natural Resource Caretaker volunteers help to preserve the more than 1,000 acres of gardens, hiking trails, pasture land and wetland. Additionally, Natural Resource Caretakers maintain trails and document wildlife. Additionally there are Living History Reenactors and Black Powder Assistant (safety officer during weapons demonstrations and reenactments). Interested people can apply online and then subsequently will have an in-person interview.

35. "LIVING HISTORY"

The Minute Man Living History Authenticity Standards is responsible for accuracy of the clothes at the park. The standards are set to most accurately depict the events of April 19, 1775 and to honor those who lost their lives in the conflict. These standards include machine stitching for clothes on seams and interior components but to finish with hand-stitching, the types and colors of fabrics used in the clothes, and objects used as props need to accurately represent the role the reenactor plays. Clothes using synthetic fabrics, modern shirts, baggy pants and breeches made from cotton for example are not allowed. Examples of where you can find "living history" exercises and demonstrations at Minute Man National Historical Park include: Hartwell Tavern, Captain William Smith House and most notably, the Parker's Revenge battle demonstration. Additionally, you will find costumed park volunteers throughout Minute Man National Historical Park who will provide interesting facts or directions. To this end, history comes to life and park visitors will remain in 1775 full time. This also shows the dedication of the re-enactors, park officials and volunteers to bringing history to life.

36. REENACTMENTS

Minute Man National Historical Park is home to some of the most accurate historical reenactments in New England and the United States. Many of these reenactments occur throughout April leading up to Patriot's Day, April 20. The top reenactments at Minute Man itself are Parker's Revenge at Battle Road and the North Bridge reenactment at Concord including a parade. During the Parker's Revenge reenactment you follow the retreating British regulars as the patriot militia harass and attack them from the woods. Walk down the trail with a crowd of spectators and truly live history as this the largest reenactment includes hundreds of volunteers dressed in British redcoats and militia-colonial clothing, horses and musket-firing. Additionally, over the month of April, you can view a Meriam's Corner reenactment which officially saw the beginning of the British retreat to Boston. You can also see the Barrett House searched by the British. Following these exercises, walk to the Paul Revere Capture Site to see a procession, reading of Longfellow's poem and finally see the capture.

37. LEXINGTON BATTLE GREEN

At 5:30 in the morning, on Patriot's Day Monday a bell rings at the Old Belfry (across from the Battle Green at Massachusetts Ave and Clarke Street) alerts the crowd of spectators and the militia of the British regular advance on Lexington. In this dramatic reenactment of April 19, 1775, see Captain John Parker assemble the town's militia and wait for the British company. As you wait in the cool morning you will eventually hear the ominous drums of the British. Then, the advance company which seemingly makes the encounter look balanced. Until the drums continue to get louder and the full British company marches into the town green, complete with horseback officers (including Pitcairn himself), bayonets and the bright-red redcoats. The militia look desperately small and unprofessional next to the British regular company. Tension fills the morning air as the British make appeals to the militia's collective common sense: "Disperse ye rebels, disperse." Soon after musket fire breaks out and the entire town square erupts in smoke and loud bangs. The battle does not last long and the militia are easily pushed back by the British.

As a kid, probably nine or ten years old, I vividly remember this day with my sister and my father. We woke up early on Patriot's Day in the black of morning to make the thirty minute drive to Lexington. I remember stopping and getting donuts and my dad drank a hot coffee; feeling the excitement of the day but also being tired and wondering why we had to wake up so early. Getting to the Lexington Green I remember the crowds of spectators of all ages waiting in the breaking-dawn for the beginning of the reenactment. First seeing the man I now know to be Captain John Parker mustering the American militia, the "good guys." Second, hearing the drums. I remember so vividly the tangible anxiety in the crowd, and myself, waiting for the engagement to begin. As the redcoats marched into the square you could not help but want to get closer, to not miss any of it. I remember it being loud and smokey. I remember being shocked that we lost, that the British advanced so easily. I remember the smells of the musket powder. I believe that morning with my dad and sister is responsible for my love of history and the American Revolution.

38. LINCOLN MINUTE MEN

The contemporary Lincoln Minute Men were founded on April 18, 1966. They include military reenactors, musicians and townspeople. They allow everyone to join including women and children 16 years or older to join and each member has a different role: Soldiers, Townspeople, Color Guard, Fifers and Drummers. The Lincoln Minute Men participate in the Paul Revere Capture reenactment, Battle Road reenactments, Concord Patriot's Day Parade crossing of the North Bridge, the Bunker Hill parade and more. At Minute Man National Historical Park they participate in "Living history" exercises and demonstrations at the Captain William Smith House. The original Lincoln Minute Men were formed in January of 1775 and were among the first to respond to the British advance at Concord.

39. LEXINGTON MINUTE MEN

The Lexington Minute Men were chartered on September 6, 1689 by the Massachusetts Governor's Council oldest militia. Today as a nonprofit organization they engage in reenactments to honor the dead and to educate about history. The Lexington

Minute Men participate in the Lexington Battle Green
reenactment, South Boston Saint Patrick's Day
Parade and more. They stand by the Minute Man
Oath: "We trust in God, that should the state of our
affairs require it, we shall be ready to sacrifice our
estates and everything dear in life, yea, and life itself
in support of the common cause." Each member
learns the biography of an actual Lexington Minute
Man who stood on Lexington Green April 19, 1775
and plays that role in reenactments. Two notable
figures that stand out to me personally are: Captain
John Parker and Ensign Robert Monroe. The earliest
ancestors of Captain Parker emigrated to the colonies
in 1609. Parker served in the French and Indian War
and would go on to lead the Lexington Minute Men
on the Green against the British. Ensign Robert
Monroe (1712-1775) served in the company and gave
his life on the Lexington Green, the morning of April
19, 1775. Like Parker, Monroe served in the French
and Indian War. Monroe, at 63 years old, was the
oldest man to give his life for the cause at the Battles
of Lexington and Concord.

A chain of command (detailed in company by-
laws) still exists within the Lexington Minute Men.
The Lexington Minute Man chain of command for
commissioned officers follows: Captain, Executive

Officer (second-in-command), Lieutenant of Muskets, Chief of Staff, Adjutant (administrative officer assistant), Lieutenant of Music, Judge Advocate (attorney serving as a member of the company), Surgeon, and Chaplains (ministers to the company). As a new recruit you will be directed by the First Lieutenant to see a company tailor for uniforms (dress and civilian clothing). The process to join is not simple: you will undergo a phone interview, in-person interview and then you will fill out an application. If successful, you will be "read in" a few months later fully joining the company. Between uniforms, musket price and company dues, this is not a cheap hobby by any means. You will find community, like-minded individuals who love history and men who want to continue the Minute Man Oath.

40. WHERE TO FIND IT

Depending on where you want to start or continue your journey of Minute Man National Park will determine the best place to park. To start at the Minute Man Visitor Center (where you will find a presentation and park guides with maps) park at 250 North Great Road, Lincoln, MA 01773. Additionally, this is the best location to park for the Patriot's Day weekend Parker's Revenge reenactments on Battle Road. You will find the North Bridge Visitor Center at 174 Liberty Street, Concord, MA 01742. Park here for the Concord Patriot's Day Parade that passes over North Bridge and includes musket firing. For Hartwell Tavern and the Bloody Angle park at Virginia Road, Lincoln, MA 01773. For parking at The Wayside and the Parker's Revenge reenactment on Patriot's Day weekend go to 174 Liberty St, Concord, MA 01742.

41. ATTRACTIONS NEARBY

Boston and its suburbs are home to American history. Three attractions to highlight in the immediate vicinity of Minute Man National Historical Park are: The Orchard House (in Concord), Bunker Hill Monument (Charlestown) and the Paul Revere House (in Boston). The Orchard House located at 399 Lexington Road, Concord, MA was home to the Alcott family and the place where Louise May Alcott wrote "Little Women." The Bunker Hill Monument stands where the battle of June 17, 1775 took place. Designated a National Historical Landmark in January of 1961, visitors can visit the Monument and

Lodge located on Breed's Hill (where the majority of the battle took place).

In Boston, find the Paul Revere House at 19 North Square. Paul Revere set off in the evening of April 18, 1775 to warn Adams and Hancock of the British regular advance. Tour his house, a National Historical Partner site. Boston, about 30 minutes or 25 miles from Lexington and Concord, is home to Faneuil Hall (built in 1742), the Freedom Trail and the Museum of Fine Arts. The Boston National Historical Park was designated a national park on October 1, 1974 and the National Park Service runs and operates it. The Boston National Historical Park connects Revolutionary War sites around Boston including the Freedom Trail, Faneuil Hall, Bunker Hill and the Paul Revere House. You cannot miss an opportunity to visit historic Boston while you are so close at Minute Man National Historical Park.

42. FEDERAL PASS PROGRAM

Annual passes are available for all National Parks. Additionally, discount passes for military (free) and youth programs available at the Minute Man Visitor Center. The America The Beautiful: National Parks &

Federal Lands Annual Pass gives the owner access to more than 2,000 federal recreation sites ($80) and is free for current U.S. military and their families. With your pass your private vehicle can enter and park and additionally, it covers the entrance fee for the pass owner and three guests.

43. WHAT TO BRING

Definitely plan your trip to Minute Man National Historical Park ahead of time! Bring water, snacks or lunch, binoculars, pet waste bags, lawn chairs (if going for a reenactment you want to arrive early). Minute Man is spread out over Lincoln, Lexington and Concord so you will want to wear comfortable sneakers for walking. If you do not feel like bringing food and want to buy some there are places to eat as well: The Concord Cheese Shop, Main Street Market and Cafe, The Colonial Inn to name a few. Be sure to pick up maps of the area available at the Minute Man Visitor Center.

44. PARK RULES

Minute Man National Historical Park is closed on holidays except for Patriot's Day. Parking lots can also be closed due to weather conditions. You need a permit to launch a drone within the park (unmanned aerial). Fishing regulated by the laws of Massachusetts, banks of the North Bridge not allowed. No electronic cigarettes. You need a Special Use Permit for a fire site. No designated area for riding horses at Minute Man but you can and are encouraged to ride on bike trails. Picnicking allowed within the park by Hartwell Tavern. Weather providing snow shoes are allowed on Battle Road Trail. You need a Special Use Permit to play recreational sports. The superintendent's office also needs to issue a permit for any kind of specimen collecting like plants or rocks. No designated camping in Minute Man. Encouraged to take lots of photos !

45. HOURS AND SEASONS OPEN

Minute Man National Historical Park is open from sunrise to sunset. The North Bridge Visitor Center is open from 9:30 a.m. to 5 p.m. throughout April leading up to Patriot's Day. The Minute Man Visitor Center is open from 9 a.m. to 5 p.m. starting in April as well. The parking lot closes at sunset. You also call Minute Man at 978-369-6993 for additional hours and tour information during off-seasons. Video program runs from 9 a.m. to 4:30 at the Minute Man Visitor Center (covering Paul Revere's Ride and the Battles of Lexington and Concord). Particular houses like the Barrett House, Smith House and the Wayside for example, have special Patriots Day weekend hours (for example on Sunday, April 19th, 1:00 - 4:00 p.m.).

46. PETS

Pets are allowed at Minute Man National Historical Park! The many trails make for great dog walking while taking in the natural beauty and history. All pets must be leashed on park property for the safety of the park visitors, volunteers and additionally, the wildlife. Pet waste must be removed as well and Minute Man does not actually provide plastic bags for waste so definitely bring your own! Pets are not allowed inside the historic buildings. While there are some restrictions, bringing your family pet to Minute Man to walk the trails will be fun and good exercise for all. On Patriot's Day weekend be sure to bring your best friend to the "Paws for a Cause" at the Minute Man Visitor Center. You will go on a 45 minute walk down Battle Road with your dog as a park employee talks about the role of dogs in the Revolutionary War. This runs from the Visitor Center to the Paul Revere Capture Site. I definitely recommend bringing your dog with you to Minute Man National Historical Park - especially if the weather looks beautiful!

47. WHERE TO STAY

You will find many accomodations in and around Lexington and Concord. Aloft Hotel (Lexington 727-A Marrett Road, Lexington, MA) and Element Lexington Hotel (727-B Marrett Road, Lexington, MA) are two upscale options only a half-mile from the park. Best Western at Historic Concord (740 Elm Street) and Concord's Colonial Inn (48 Memorial Square) will definitely serve as the best option to stay near the Old North Bridge area of Minute Man. The Inn at Hastings Park Lexington (2027 Massachusetts Ave, Lexington, MA) is another affordable option. You'll want to get a room close to the Lexington

Town Green to get a front row spot for the Battle of Lexington Patriot's Day reenactment which of course starts at 5:30 in the morning!

48. FRIENDS OF MINUTE MAN NATIONAL HISTORICAL PARK

Independent non-profit organization. Supports the park through education, fundraising and hosting events. The two major ways they support the park are: Battlefield Restoration and Landscape Preservation. The Friends of Minute Men do great work for example at the Parker's Revenge site they uncovered 29 musket balls. Friends of Minute Man also help trail preservation along the battlefield. Another important aspect of their work concerns landscape preservation. Buttrick Gardens is 6 acres and overlooks Concord's North Bridge.

49. BIKING

Biking is very popular at Minute Man National Historical Park. Battle Road Trail runs for 5 miles. To bike here park along Route 2A and Lexington Road for best access. It goes from Fiske Hill to Meriam's

Corner, the "Battle Road Unit" of Minute Man. You will ride across mild hills with no steep inclines making it an easy ride. A boardwalk allows riders to pass over wetlands in two sections of the trail. Running close to Minute Man National Historical Park is the Minuteman Bikeway, a 10 mile multi-use paved trail built by the Commonwealth of Massachusetts. It follows original railroad lines for steam engines and was fully converted to a bike trail in 1991. The Minuteman Bikeway stretches from Bedford to Alewife to Cambridge and passes through Lexington and Concord and follows Paul Revere's ride on April 18, 1775.

50. WHY YOU NEED TO GO

I believe all Americans should see where the birth of their nation began. It would be incorrect to think the American Revolution solely began in Massachusetts, but the first colonists to stand against "Taxation without representation" and the first to form lines against the British regulars were right here in Lexington and Concord. Minute Man National Historical Park brings history to life in a way that not many other institutions can do. Lexington and

Concord are home to much more than just the birthplace of the American Revolution. The "Home of the Authors" the Wayside links literary legends like Henry David Thoreau and Louise May Alcott. The Robbins House shows its visitors how the first freed generations of African Americans lived. Relive the history made on April 19, 1775. As you walk down Battle Road Trail feel the fear of the retreating British seeing the smoke break out in the woods as patriot militia ambush them at Parker's Revenge. With reenactments, park volunteers who engage with visitors and the natural beauty of Lincoln, Lexington and Concord, you cannot miss an opportunity to visit Minute Man National Historical Park.

TOP REASONS TO BOOK THIS TRIP

History - walk the same roads as the patriots who sparked the American Revolution and see where many made the ultimate sacrifice.

Natural Beauty - enjoy Minute Man's natural landscape, animals and plants.

Immersive - through reenactments feel, see and touch history.

OTHER RESOURCES:

https://www.nps.gov/mima/index.htm

https://www.history.com/topics/american-
revolution/american-revolution-history

https://www.lexingtonma.gov/

https://www.concordma.gov/

"Boston and the American Revolution": Official
National Park Handbook. National Park Service
© August 1998.

"Lexington and Concord: The Battle Heard Round
the World" by George C. Daughan. W.W. Norton
& Co © April 2018

PACKING AND PLANNING TIPS

A Week before Leaving

- Arrange for someone to take care of pets and water plants.

- Email and Print important Documents.

- Get Visa and vaccines if needed.

- Check for travel warnings.

- Stop mail and newspaper.

- Notify Credit Card companies where you are going.

- Passports and photo identification is up to date.

- Pay bills.

- Copy important items and download travel Apps.

- Start collecting small bills for tips.

- Have post office hold mail while you are away.

- Check weather for the week.

- Car inspected, oil is changed, and tires have the correct pressure.

- Check airline luggage restrictions.

- Download Apps needed for your trip.

Right Before Leaving

- Contact bank and credit cards to tell them your location.

- Clean out refrigerator.

- Empty garbage cans.

- Lock windows.

- Make sure you have the proper identification with you.

- Bring cash for tips.

- Remember travel documents.

- Lock door behind you.

- Remember wallet.

- Unplug items in house and pack chargers.

- Change your thermostat settings.

- Charge electronics, and prepare camera memory cards.

READ OTHER
GREATER THAN A TOURIST
BOOKS

Greater Than a Tourist- Geneva Switzerland: 50 Travel Tips from a Local by Amalia Kartika

Greater Than a Tourist- St. Croix US Birgin Islands USA: 50 Travel Tips from a Local by Tracy Birdsall

Greater Than a Tourist- San Juan Puerto Rico: 50 Travel Tips from a Local by Melissa Tait

Greater Than a Tourist – Lake George Area New York USA: 50 Travel Tips from a Local by Janine Hirschklau

Greater Than a Tourist – Monterey California United States: 50 Travel Tips from a Local by Katie Begley

Greater Than a Tourist – Chanai Crete Greece: 50 Travel Tips from a Local by Dimitra Papagrigoraki

Greater Than a Tourist – The Garden Route Western Cape Province South Africa: 50 Travel Tips from a Local by Li-Anne McGregor van Aardt

Greater Than a Tourist – Sevilla Andalusia Spain: 50 Travel Tips from a Local by Gabi Gazon

Children's Book: *Charlie the Cavalier Travels the World* by Lisa Rusczyk Ed. D.

> TOURIST

Follow us on Instagram for beautiful travel images:
http://Instagram.com/GreaterThanATourist

Follow *Greater Than a Tourist* on Amazon.

>Tourist Podcast

>T Website

>T Youtube

>T Facebook

>T Goodreads

>T Amazon

>T Mailing List

>T Pinterest

>T Instagram

>T Twitter

>T SoundCloud

>T LinkedIn

>T Map

> TOURIST

At *Greater Than a Tourist,* we love to share travel tips with you. How did we do? What guidance do you have for how we can give you better advice for your next trip? Please send your feedback to GreaterThanaTourist@gmail.com as we continue to improve the series. We appreciate your constructive feedback. Thank you.

METRIC CONVERSIONS

TEMPERATURE

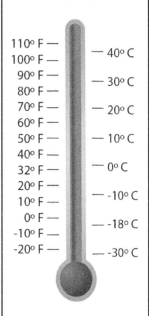

110° F —   — 40° C
100° F —
90° F —   — 30° C
80° F —
70° F —   — 20° C
60° F —
50° F —   — 10° C
40° F —
32° F —   — 0° C
20° F —
10° F —   — -10° C
0° F —
-10° F —   — -18° C
-20° F —   — -30° C

To convert F to C:

Subtract 32, and then multiply by 5/9 or .5555.

To Convert C to F:

Multiply by 1.8 and then add 32.

32F = 0C

LIQUID VOLUME

To Convert:..................Multiply by
U.S. Gallons to Liters............... 3.8
U.S. Liters to Gallons 26
Imperial Gallons to U.S. Gallons 1.2
Imperial Gallons to Liters....... 4.55
Liters to Imperial Gallons 22
1 Liter = .26 U.S. Gallon
1 U.S. Gallon = 3.8 Liters

DISTANCE

To convert ....Multiply by
Inches to Centimeters 2.54
Centimeters to Inches 39
Feet to Meters...................... .3
Meters to Feet 3.28
Yards to Meters 91
Meters to Yards 1.09
Miles to Kilometers 1.61
Kilometers to Miles............ .62
1 Mile = 1.6 km
1 km = .62 Miles

WEIGHT

1 Ounce = .28 Grams
1 Pound = .4555 Kilograms
1 Gram = .04 Ounce
1 Kilogram = 2.2 Pounds

TRAVEL QUESTIONS

- Do you bring presents home to family or friends after a vacation?

- Do you get motion sick?

- Do you have a favorite billboard?

- Do you know what to do if there is a flat tire?

- Do you like a sun roof open?

- Do you like to eat in the car?

- Do you like to wear sun glasses in the car?

- Do you like toppings on your ice cream?

- Do you use public bathrooms?

- Did you bring a cell phone and does it have power?

- Do you have a form of identification with you?

- Have you ever been pulled over by a cop?

- Have you ever given money to a stranger on a road trip?

- Have you ever taken a road trip with animals?

- Have you ever gone on a vacation alone?

- Have you ever run out of gas?

- If you could move to any place in the world, where would it be?

- If you could travel anywhere in the world, where would you travel?

- If you could travel in any vehicle, which one would it be?

- If you had three things to wish for from a magic genie, what would they be?

- If you have a driver's license, how many times did it take you to pass the test?

- What are you the most afraid of on vacation?

- What do you want to get away from the most when you are on vacation?

- What foods smell bad to you?

- What item do you bring on ever trip with you away from home?

- What makes you sleepy?

- What song would you love to hear on the radio when you're cruising on the highway?

- What travel job would you want the least?

- What will you miss most while you are away from home?

- What is something you always wanted to try?

- What is the best road side attraction that you ever saw?

- What is the farthest distance you ever biked?

- What is the farthest distance you ever walked?

- What is the weirdest thing you needed to buy while on vacation?

- What is your favorite candy?

- What is your favorite color car?

- What is your favorite family vacation?

- What is your favorite food?

- What is your favorite gas station drink or food?

- What is your favorite license plate design?

- What is your favorite restaurant?

- What is your favorite smell?

- What is your favorite song?

- What is your favorite sound that nature makes?

- What is your favorite thing to bring home from a vacation?

- What is your favorite vacation with friends?

- What is your favorite way to relax?

- Where is the farthest place you ever traveled in a car?

- Where is the farthest place you ever went North, South, East and West?

- Where is your favorite place in the world?

- Who is your favorite singer?

- Who taught you how to drive?

- Who will you miss the most while you are away?

- Who if the first person you will contact when you get to your destination?

- Who brought you on your first vacation?

- Who likes to travel the most in your life?

- Would you rather be hot or cold?

- Would you rather drive above, below, or at the speed limited?

- Would you rather drive on a highway or a back road?

- Would you rather go on a train or a boat?

- Would you rather go to the beach or the woods?

TRAVEL BUCKET LIST

1.

2.

3.

4.

5.

6.

7.

8.

9.

10.

NOTES